LUKA MODRIĆ

BY MICHAEL DECKER

WORLD'S GREATEST SOCCER PLAYERS

SportsZone

An Imprint of Abdo Publishing
abdobooks.com

abdobooks.com

Published by Abdo Publishing, a division of ABDO, PO Box 398166, Minneapolis, Minnesota 55439.

Printed in China
082019
012020

THIS BOOK CONTAINS
RECYCLED MATERIALS

Cover Photo: Paul White/AP Images
Interior Photos: Frank Hoermann/Sven Simon/picture-alliance/dpa/AP Images, 4; Martin Meissner/AP Images, 7; Gregorio Borgia/AP Images, 8–9; AFP/Getty Images, 10; Christof Stache/AP Images, 12; Tom Hevezi/AP Images, 15; Andy Wong/AP Images, 16; Matt Dunham/AP Images, 19; Andres Kudacki/AP Images, 20–21; Paulo Duarte/AP Images, 22; Sergei Grits/AP Images, 24, 26–27; Cezaro De Luca/picture-alliance/dpa/AP Images, 29

Editor: Patrick Donnelly
Series Designer: Craig Hinton

Library of Congress Control Number: 2019942090

Publisher's Cataloging-in-Publication Data

Names: Decker, Michael, author.
Title: Luka Modrić / by Michael Decker
Description: Minneapolis, Minnesota : Abdo Publishing, 2020 | Series: World's greatest soccer players | Includes online resources and index.
Identifiers: ISBN 9781532190643 (lib. bdg.) | ISBN 9781644943434 (pbk.) | ISBN 9781532176494 (ebook)
Subjects: LCSH: Soccer players--Biography--Juvenile literature. | Real Madrid (Soccer team)--Juvenile literature. | European football--Biography--Juvenile literature. | Professional athletes--Biography--Juvenile literature.
Classification: DDC 796.3340922--dc23

TABLE OF CONTENTS

CHAPTER
ONE

A RUN FOR THE CUP

The opening was there for Luka Modrić. The Croatia midfielder surveyed the field. He saw teammate Ante Rebić had a chance to make a run at the Denmark goal. So Modrić passed the ball to the space just ahead of Rebić. Now Rebić had the ball and a clear path in front of him. Just then, a defender brought him down. The referee blew his whistle and awarded Croatia a penalty kick.

This was a big moment. Denmark and Croatia were playing in the 2018 World Cup round of 16. The score was even at 1–1. Only four minutes remained in extra time.

Luka Modrić had an eventful day when Croatia met Denmark in the 2018 World Cup.

Modrić's pass had helped set up this penalty kick. Now the Croatia manager selected Modrić to take the kick.

Modrić knew this was his chance to be the hero. A goal would likely win the game. Using his right foot, he drilled a shot toward the right side of the net. But Denmark goalkeeper Kasper Schmeichel was there. He dived for the ball, stopped it with his hand, and brought it in for a save. Modrić stared into space in disbelief. But there was no time to sulk. The teams played on.

After more than 30 minutes of extra time, the match was still tied. A shootout would decide the winner. Modrić, the team captain, was still upset about his earlier miss. He told the Croatia manager he wanted a chance to redeem himself with another penalty kick.

Modrić shot third for Croatia. His team trailed 2–1 in the shootout. Modrić again shot with his right foot. Schmeichel guessed the ball would again go to his left, so he dove that way. Instead, this time Modrić kicked the ball to the center of the net. It zipped past the goalie's

Kasper Schmeichel, *in yellow*, makes the save on a Modrić penalty kick late in extra time.

feet and into the net. Moments later, teammate Ivan Rakitić converted his shot, too. That was all Croatia needed to pull out a win over Denmark to advance to the World Cup quarterfinals.

It surprised many that Croatia was still alive in the tournament. It was one of the smaller countries to qualify for the World Cup. But it was less surprising that Modrić was leading the way. The playmaking midfielder was a star for his club team, Real Madrid. Now he was leading his country on a historic run. And Croatia wasn't done yet.

LEADING THE WAY

Modrić was a star for Croatia in the 2018 World Cup knockout round. But he also made other key plays for Croatia during the group stage. In three matches, Modrić scored two goals. He helped his team go 3–0, earning first place in Group D and qualifying Croatia for the knockout round.

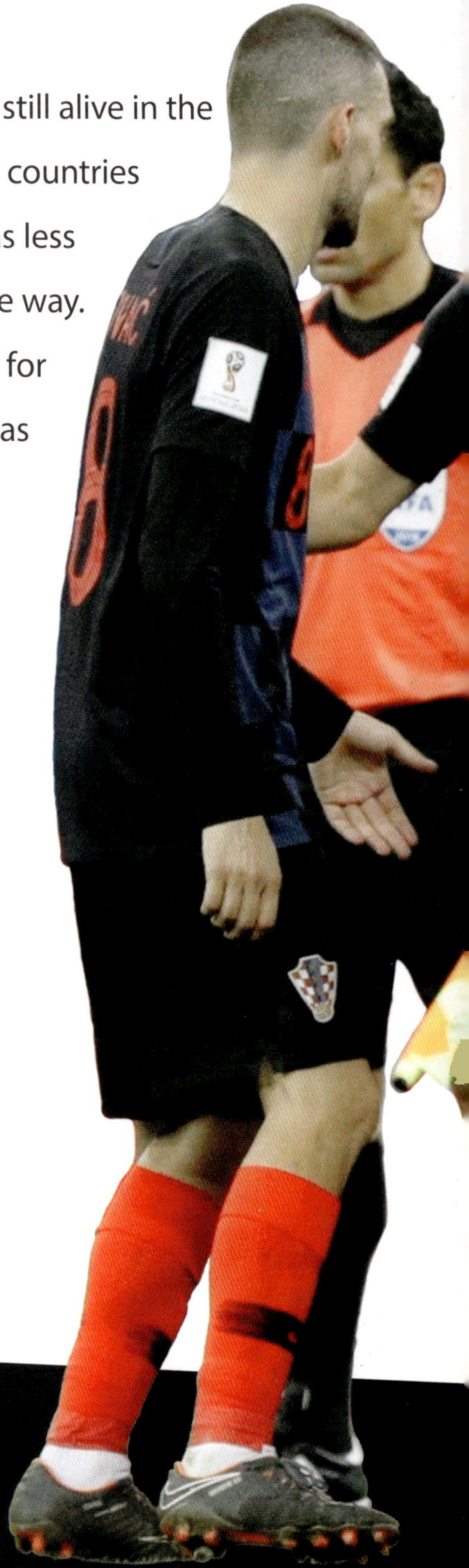

Modrić (10) is congratulated by his teammates after successfully converting his penalty kick during the shootout.

22
MODRIĆ
10

NK ZADAR
NK ZADAR
Hrvoje Ćustić

CHAPTER
TWO

A YOUNG **TALENT**

Luka Modrić was born in Modrići, Croatia, on September 9, 1985. When Luka was a child, Croatia fought a war for its independence. People were being killed around his family's village. The family moved to Zadar, a larger city on the Adriatic Sea, to avoid the violence.

Luka was six years old when his family moved to Zadar. He spent hours a day kicking a soccer ball. Many Croatian children tried to distract themselves from the war by playing soccer. That time playing paid off for Luka as he developed into a very skilled soccer player.

Luka began his soccer career playing for his hometown club, NK Zadar.

14

Luka started on his hometown youth team, NK Zadar. At 15 he was signed by Dinamo Zagreb, a top club team in Croatia. This move meant Luka was officially a professional soccer player.

Luka played in the midfield, where he showed his great vision and playmaking abilities. From 2005 to 2007, Luka helped Dinamo to three consecutive league titles. He was named the league's player of the year in 2007.

At the same time, Luka was starting to have success with Croatia's national team. He made his national team debut in March 2006. That summer he played in the 2006 World Cup.

HIS SPORTING FATHER

Tomislav Bašić was one of Luka's first coaches at NK Zadar. Bašić became a mentor for Luka. When Luka was 15, Bašić negotiated his contract with Dinamo Zagreb. Today, Luka considers Bašić to be his second father.

Luka was just 20 when he played his first match with Croatia's national team.

Some bigger European clubs began to notice Luka and tried to convince him to join their team. But he wanted to stay in Croatia. When he was 22 years old, Luka finally decided it was time to move away from his own country and compete against the best players in the world.

In April 2008, he agreed to join Tottenham Hotspur of the English Premier League. The transfer fee of $33 million matched a Spurs team record. Tottenham fans were curious to find out more about their new player. And while he might not have made an immediate impact, he would soon become a fan favorite.

Modrić was ready for a bigger challenge when he signed with Tottenham Hotspur in 2008.

MODRIĆ
14

CHAPTER
THREE

MAKING AN IMPACT

England's Premier League is one of the most competitive leagues in the world. It's also a very physical league. At first Modrić struggled there. At just 5 feet 8 inches (1.7 m) and 145 pounds (66 kg), Modrić had to show he could keep up. Injuries didn't help, either. Some fans wondered if Modrić had what it took to succeed in England.

By his second season, in 2009–10, questions about his fitness for the Premier League disappeared. Modrić became a key player for Tottenham. He showed his versatility playing center midfielder and left wing.

Modrić had to get accustomed to the physical style of the Premier League.

Modrić was at his best at center midfield, where he could control more of what was happening on offense.

Many bigger teams were eager to sign him. But Modrić decided to stay with Tottenham, signing a new contract in 2010. He wanted to help the club improve.

That showed in the 2010–11 season, when the club reached the European Champions League quarterfinals. It was the first time Tottenham had ever qualified to play in the Champions League. Modrić was most effective as a passer. He averaged 62.5 passes per match, more than any other Spurs player.

But after four seasons with Tottenham, Modrić was ready for a bigger stage. In 2012 he signed with Real Madrid, one of the top clubs in Spain's La Liga and the world. At first Modrić struggled to find playing time. Real Madrid had veteran players at midfield. Modrić mainly played as a substitute.

Modrić, *right*, helped Tottenham defeat AC Milan to reach the Champions League quarterfinals in 2011.

Modrić eventually started to make a bigger impact for Real Madrid. In a December 2012 match, Modrić assisted on two goals in a 4–1 victory. Many more key

RONALDO
7

plays followed. Modrić's precise passing helped set up his talented teammates to score.

Though some of his teammates were more famous, Modrić became a fan favorite as he led Real Madrid on an amazing run.

A TALE OF TWO TEAMS

Modrić played for two clubs with different Champions League histories. Tottenham reached the quarterfinals in 2010–11, the first time it had ever qualified for the Champions League. On the other hand, Real Madrid won the first five titles from 1956 through 1960 and captured its record thirteenth title in 2018.

In Madrid Modrić teamed with other world superstars including Cristiano Ronaldo, *left*, and Mesut Özil.

CHAPTER
FOUR

ONE OF THE BEST

By the 2013–14 season, Modrić was a regular starter for Real Madrid. The team was loaded with superstars. Modrić helped bring everyone together. His play was key in helping Real Madrid reach the Champions League final.

Real Madrid faced rival Atlético Madrid for the European title. Atlético led 1–0 late into the game. Then Modrić set up a late goal off a corner kick to tie the score 1–1. That sent the match to extra time, where Real Madrid posted a flurry of goals to win 4–1. The club had won its tenth Champions League title.

Modrić rides the shoulders of teammate Alvaro Arbeloa as they celebrate Real Madrid's victory in the 2014 Champions League final.

Injuries kept Modrić from helping Croatia advance in the 2014 World Cup.

In 2014 Modrić was back in the World Cup with Croatia. The Croatian fans expected a lot from him and the team. However, Modrić battled numerous injuries and Croatia struggled, losing two of its three group matches and failing to reach the knockout round.

Those struggles didn't carry over to Real Madrid, who won another Champions League title in 2016, again with Modrić as a regular in the starting lineup. This was the start of an exciting run for Real Madrid. The next year Modrić set up teammate Cristiano Ronaldo for a goal in the final as Real Madrid won its second consecutive Champions League crown. Then the club made it three consecutive titles in 2018.

THE FIRST RUN

Before helping Croatia to the 2018 World Cup final, Modrić was a 12-year-old in his home country watching Croatia compete in the 1998 World Cup. In its first World Cup, Croatia advanced all the way to the semifinals before losing to France, the eventual champion. Modrić said that team inspired him to play for the Croatian national team one day.

Fans saw what Modrić could do with Real Madrid. His Croatia team had a lot of talent, too. Still, few expected they would make such a long run at the 2018 World Cup.

After all, they were drawn into a tough group that included Argentina, Iceland, and Nigeria. Along with teammates Mario Mandžukić and Ivan Rakitić, Modrić led Croatia on a run. They won all three group-stage games. Then Croatia beat Denmark, and wins against host Russia as well as England followed after that. Just like that, the tiny country of 4 million people was in the World Cup final.

After that, Modrić was no longer overshadowed by more famous teammates. He played a central role for Croatia. And even though they fell to France 4–2 in the final, they had gone on one of the most unlikely runs in World Cup history.

Modrić and Real Madrid defeated Liverpool in 2018 for its third straight Champions League title.

Though his team came in second, Modrić was recognized for his excellence in the tournament by winning the Golden Ball. That trophy goes to the best player in the World Cup. To cap off the year, Modrić won the Ballon d'Or, the annual award given to the top soccer player in the world. With his success at the World Cup and with Real Madrid, Modrić has become one of the most decorated soccer players in the game today.

Though it wasn't the trophy he wanted, Modrić did receive the Golden Ball, given to the best player in the 2018 World Cup.

GLOSSARY

Champions League

A competition for the best soccer clubs from the various European leagues.

club

The team a player competes with outside of his or her national team.

contract

An agreement to play for a certain team.

corner kick

A free kick from a corner of the field that is awarded when the ball goes out of bounds over the end line and is last touched by the defense.

debut

First appearance.

extra time

Two 15-minute periods added to a game when the score is tied at the end of regulation.

group stage

The part of a tournament when teams are divided into smaller groups or pools; each team faces the others in group, and those with the best records move on to the knockout stage.

knockout round

The part of a tournament in which one loss eliminates a team.

midfielder

A player who stays mostly in the middle third of the field and links the defenders with the forwards.

penalty kick

A play in which a shooter faces a goalkeeper alone; it is used to decide tie games or as a result of a defensive foul near the goal.

rival

An opponent with whom a player or team has a fierce and ongoing competition.

MORE INFORMATION

BOOKS

Avise, Jonathan. *Champions League Legends*. Minneapolis, MN: Abdo Publishing, 2019.

Kortemeier, Todd. *Make Me the Best Soccer Player*. Minneapolis, MN: Abdo Publishing, 2017.

Kortemeier, Todd. *Real Madrid CF*. Minneapolis, MN: Abdo Publishing, 2018.

ONLINE RESOURCES

Booklinks
NONFICTION NETWORK
FREE! ONLINE NONFICTION RESOURCES

To learn more about Luka Modrić, please visit **abdobooklinks.com** or scan this QR code. These links are routinely monitored and updated to provide the most current information available.

INDEX

ABOUT THE AUTHOR

Originally from a small town in the Upper Peninsula of Michigan, Michael Decker has spent his career as a children's book author, writing about various sports such as soccer. He lives in Laramie, Wyoming, with his wife, three kids, and his dog, Emily.